THE OFFICIAL
ARSENAL FC
Maths Book 1
Paul Broadbent

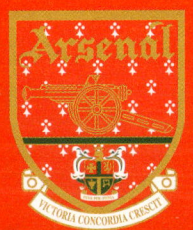

Gunning for Goals

Education is essential to everyone and basic skills such as English and Maths are vitally important to every child's development.

Teaching core subjects through sport, I feel, is the best way. Encouraging youngsters to reach their goals in the classroom through Arsenal based activities is both a motivational and rewarding exercise.

That's why the Club already spearheads a number of successful education initiatives, including after school learning programmes at the Arsenal Study Support Centre and through the Arsenal 'Double Club'.

The inception of the Official Arsenal FC Workbook series further illustrates the Club's commitment to education. More importantly these books present an interesting and fun approach to learning at home.

I hope this book motivates you to accomplish your goals.

Arsène Wenger

Arsenal Study Support Centre
28 Carleton Road
London N7 0EQ
stevewilson@arsenalstudysupport.org
Telephone 020 7697 8467
Fax 020 7697 0873

Arsenal Double Club
Arsenal Stadium
London N5 1BU
bnicholas@arsenal.co.uk
Telephone 020 7704 4140
Fax 020 7704 4101

Kick-off

The Arsenal FC books are a fun way to learn and practise your Maths skills. Each book contains:
Theme visits to Arsenal FC, six Big Matches and a board game!

The 'theme' visits

Learn more about Arsenal FC and football.

Enjoy the fun activities (*answers on pages 30–31*).

The Big Matches

Learn a new skill.

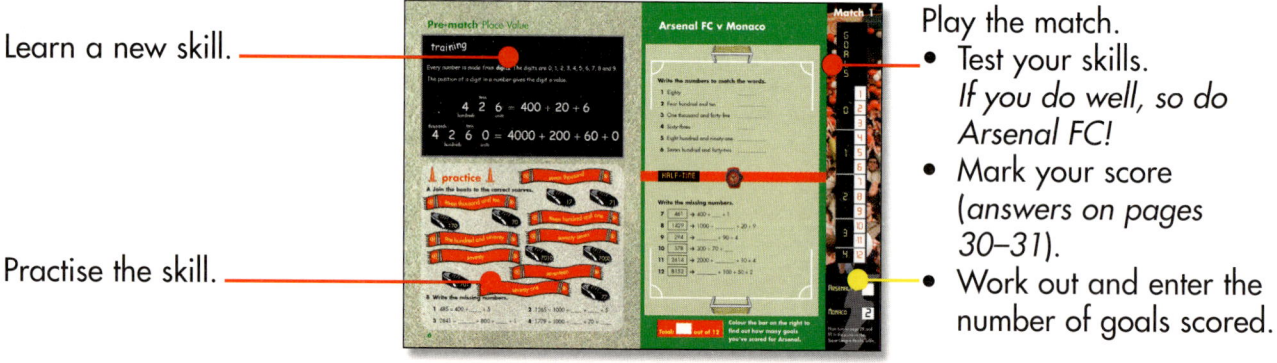

Play the match.
- Test your skills. *If you do well, so do Arsenal FC!*
- Mark your score (*answers on pages 30–31*).
- Work out and enter the number of goals scored.

Practise the skill.

After the match:
Enter each result on page 28. Work out Arsenal FC's league position!

The board game

What you need.

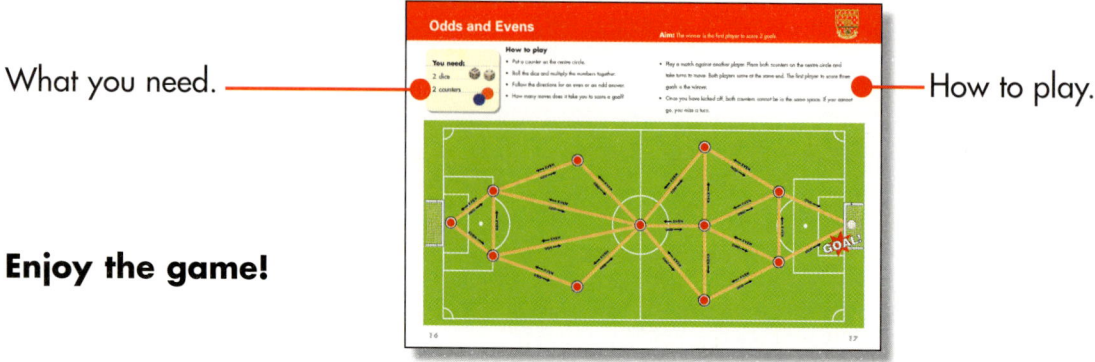

How to play.

Enjoy the game!

2

Contents

	page		page
The Club	4	**Highbury**	20
Match 1 Place Value	6	**Match 5** Time	22
The Players	8	**The Team**	24
Match 2 Addition and Subtraction	10	**Match 6** Rounding and Reading Scales	26
The Strip	12	**Super-League Tables**	28
Match 3 Multiplication Tables	14	**Answers**	30
Odds and Evens	16	**Information**	32
Match 4 Money	18		

3

The Club

The chart on the right shows some important dates in the history of Arsenal FC. Answer these questions.

1. How many years after they joined the football league did Arsenal win their first League Championship? 12
2. How many times have Arsenal won the FA Cup? 10
3. How many names have they had? 3
4. In what year did manager Arsène Wenger join Arsenal? _____
5. How many years are there between their first and second league doubles? _____

Use the code on the scarf to find out the answers.

F	O	O	T	B	A	L	L
6	15	15	20	2	1	12	12

ADD UP ALL THESE NUMBERS

'FOOTBALL' SCORES 83 POINTS

6. What is the total number of points scored by ARSENAL?

A	R	S	E	N	A	L
1	18	19	5	14	1	12

total _____

Did you know ... ?
Arsenal used to be known as The Reds, but now their nickname is The Gunners.

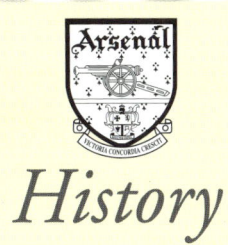

History

Year	Event
1886	Workers from the Woolwich Arsenal Armament Factory form a football club first called Dial Square, then Royal Arsenal
1891	The club turned professional and changed its name to Woolwich Arsenal
1893	Joined the football league
1930	Arsenal win their first of seven FA Cups
1931	Arsenal win their first League Championship title
1971	Double winners: League Championship and FA Cup
1987	First League Cup win
1994	Victory in Europe with the European Cup Winners' Cup
1996	Arsène Wenger becomes the club's manager
1998	Arsenal win the second double of their history

Herbert Chapman

Here are some important dates in the history of Arsenal FC.

7 Find the points scored by these teams.

MANCHESTER UNITED Total _____

CHELSEA Total _____

NEWCASTLE UNITED Total _____

LIVERPOOL Total _____

8 Add up the points scored by Dennis Bergkamp and then by Thierry Henry. Whose total is greater?

139

175

_____

5

Pre-match Place Value

training

Every number is made from **digits**. The digits are 0, 1, 2, 3, 4, 5, 6, 7, 8 and 9.

The position of a digit in a number gives the digit a value.

4 (hundreds) 2 (tens) 6 (units) = 400 + 20 + 6

4 (thousands) 2 (hundreds) 6 (tens) 0 (units) = 4000 + 200 + 60 + 0

practice

A Join the boots to the correct scarves.

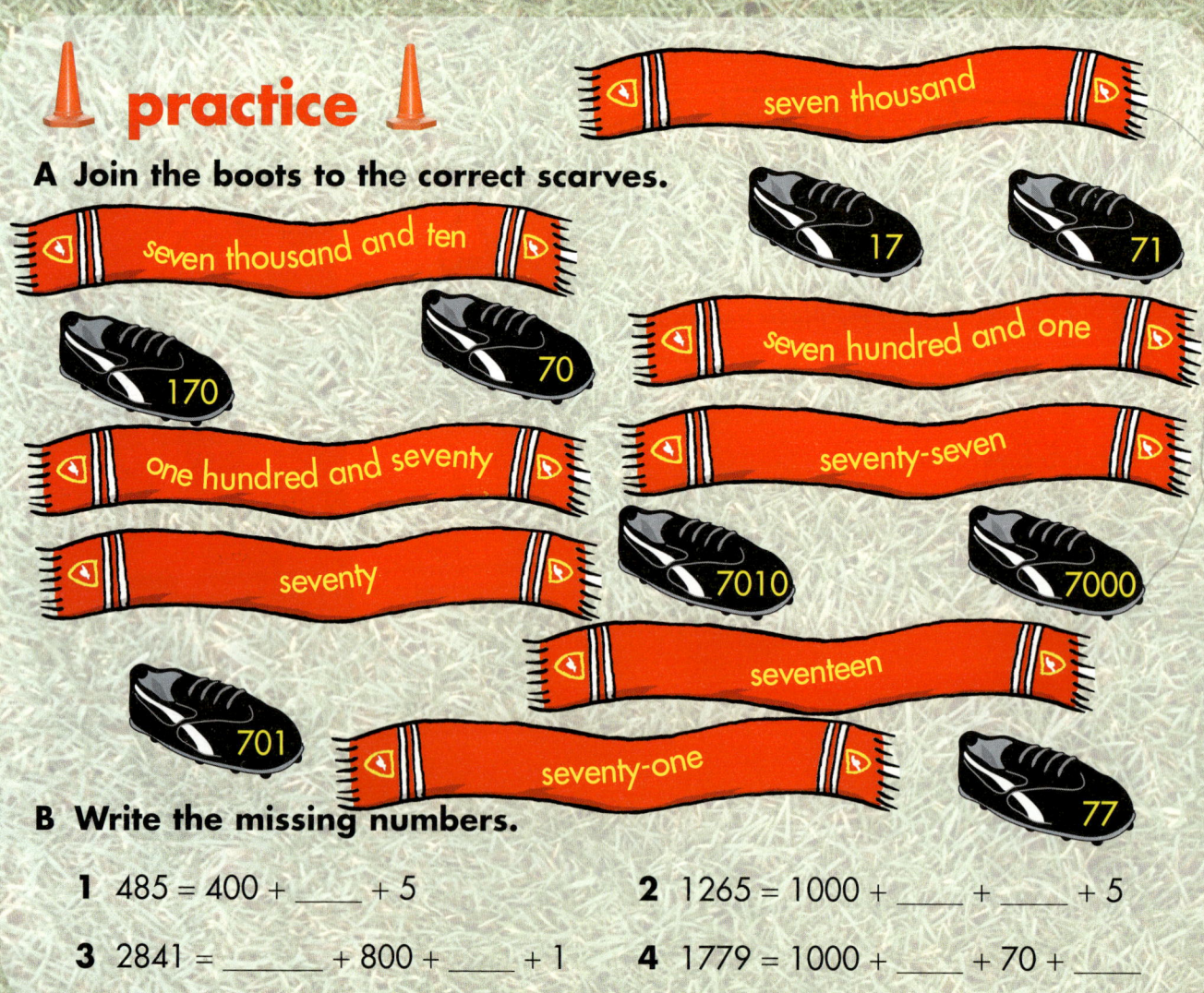

B Write the missing numbers.

1 485 = 400 + ____ + 5

2 1265 = 1000 + ____ + ____ + 5

3 2841 = ____ + 800 + ____ + 1

4 1779 = 1000 + ____ + 70 + ____

Arsenal FC v Monaco

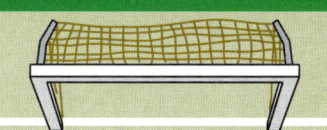

Write the numbers to match the words.

1. Eighty — 80
2. Four hundred and ten — 410
3. One thousand and forty-five — 1045
4. Sixty-three — 63
5. Eight hundred and ninety-one — 891
6. Seven hundred and forty-two — 742

HALF-TIME

Write the missing numbers.

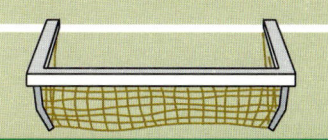

7. 461 → 400 + 60 + 1
8. 1429 → 1000 + 400 + 20 + 9
9. 294 → 200 + 90 + 4
10. 378 → 300 + 70 + 8
11. 2614 → 2000 + 600 + 10 + 4
12. 8152 → 8000 + 100 + 50 + 2

Total: ___ out of 12

Colour the bar on the right to find out how many goals you've scored for Arsenal.

Match 1

GOALS

Arsenal FC: ___
Monaco: 2

Now turn to page 28 and fill in the score on the Super-League Results Table.

The Players

Do you share a birthday with any of these players?

Happy Birthday Arsenal!

David Seaman	19 September	Ray Parlour	7 March
John Lukic	11 December	Silvinho	12 April
Alex Manninger	4 June	Gilles Grimandi	11 November
Stuart Taylor	28 November	Stefan Malz	15 June
Lee Dixon	17 March	Matthew Upson	18 April
Igors Stepanovs	21 January	Oleg Luzhny	5 August
Patrick Vieira	23 June	Nelson Vivas	18 October
Martin Keown	24 July	Kanu	1 August
Tony Adams	10 October	Graham Barrett	6 October
Robert Pires	29 January	Ashley Cole	20 December
Fredrik Ljungberg	16 April	And the Manager...	
Dennis Bergkamp	10 May	Arsène Wenger	22 October
Sylvain Wiltord	10 May		
Lauren	19 January		
Thierry Henry	17 August		

The grid shows the initials of some of the 2000/2001 squad.

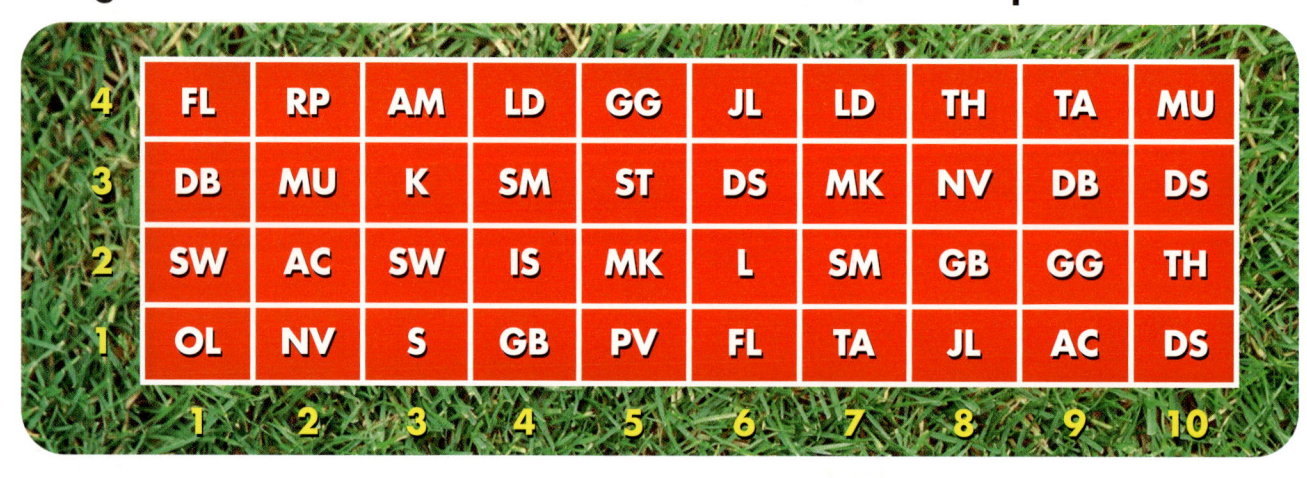

4	FL	RP	AM	LD	GG	JL	LD	TH	TA	MU
3	DB	MU	K	SM	ST	DS	MK	NV	DB	DS
2	SW	AC	SW	IS	MK	L	SM	GB	GG	TH
1	OL	NV	S	GB	PV	FL	TA	JL	AC	DS
	1	2	3	4	5	6	7	8	9	10

2 Thierry Henry (TH) is at position (10,2). What other position(s) can you find him in?

_____

3 Can you find other players who are in two or more positions on the grid?

Give their surnames and positions. _____

_____

_____

8

Month	Number of Birthdays
	1 2 3 4 5 6
January	
February	
March	
April	
May	
June	
July	
August	
September	
October	
November	
December	

1 Complete this bar chart. Find the month when no Arsenal player has a birthday.

_____

4 Use the grid of players' initials to complete this crossword of their surnames.

Across
1 (6,3), 4 (8,1), 6 (9,4)
8 (2,4), 9 (10,2), 10 (5,1)
11 (4,3)

Down
1 (4,2), 2 (1,3), 3 (2,2)
4 (6,2), 5 (3,3), 7 (3,1)

5 Who is the hidden former Arsenal favourite and current Leeds United manager? Rearrange the coloured letters on the crossword to find out. _____

Pre-match Addition and Subtraction

training

Learn these **addition** words:

ALTOGETHER	sum
add	TOTAL	more than
greater than	PLUS

Learn these **subtraction** words:

less than	difference
subtract	MINUS	take away
fewer than	LEAVES

When you **add** numbers the order **does not** matter.
2 + 15 has the **same** answer as 15 + 2.

When you **subtract** numbers the order **does** matter.
15 − 6 **does not have the same** answer as 6 − 15.

practice

A Total these pairs.

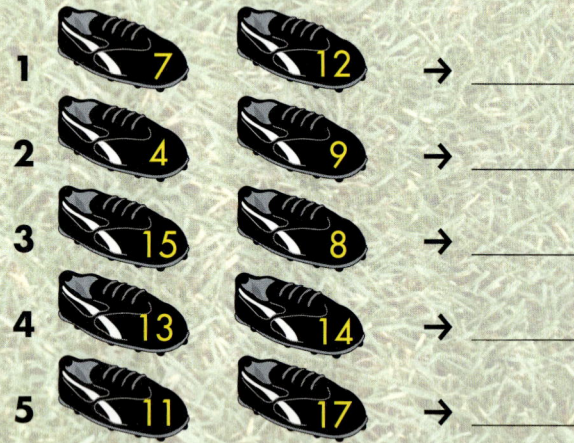

1. 7, 12 → _____
2. 4, 9 → _____
3. 15, 8 → _____
4. 13, 14 → _____
5. 11, 17 → _____

Find the difference between these pairs.

6. 9, 15 → _____
7. 18, 13 → _____
8. 14, 17 → _____
9. 6, 19 → _____
10. 13, 5 → _____

B 1 What is the sum of 5 and 13?

2 What is the total of 7, 9 and 4?

3 Which number is 6 less than 17?

4 What is 19 subtract 5?

Arsenal FC v Lazio

Match 2

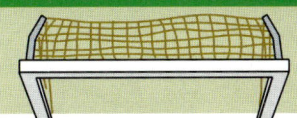

Work out these.

1. 19 + 4 = 13
2. 14 − 6 = ____
3. 8 + 9 + 5 = ____
4. 17 − 8 = ____
5. 15 + 18 = ____
6. 3 + 14 + 7 = ____

HALF-TIME

Try these.

7. What is the sum of 15 and 6? ____
8. Which number is 12 less than 20? ____
9. What is the total of 8, 9 and 10? ____
10. Mark and Anna spend 16p each. How much do they spend altogether? ____
11. Sam has 14 badges and Jack has 7 more. How many badges does Jack have? ____
12. Rebecca has 18 sweets. She eats 6 and gives 8 to David. How many sweets does she have left? ____

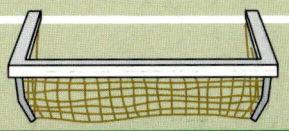

Total: ☐ **out of 12**

Colour the bar on the right to find out how many goals you've scored for Arsenal.

GOALS

0	1
	2
	3
1	4
	5
	6
2	7
	8
	9
3	10
	11
4	12

ARSENAL FC ☐

LAZIO 3

Now turn to page 28 and fill in the score on the Super-League Results Table.

The Strip

Arsenal started off as amateurs and they had very little money for a kit. Two players who had come from Nottingham asked Nottingham Forest for some shirts, which is why they play in red.

The kit's distinctive white sleeves and collar were added in 1933 to set the kit apart from the other football teams that played in red. They have kept the same colours ever since.

Sorting out socks.

3 The socks scattered on the right are muddled up. Join the matching pairs.

4 Circle the socks to help you to work out these fractions.

    a $\frac{1}{2}$ of 8 = _____   **b** $\frac{1}{4}$ of 12 = _____   **c** $\frac{1}{2}$ of 10 = _____

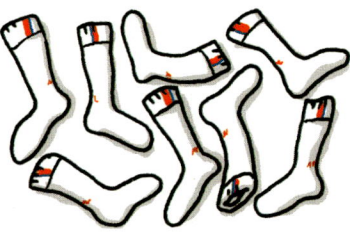 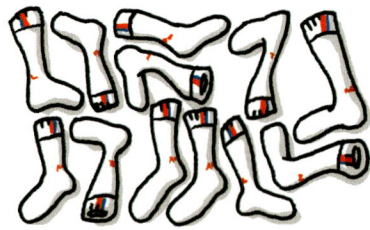 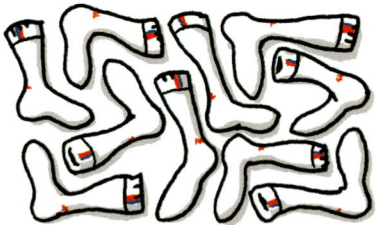

    d $\frac{1}{3}$ of 12 = _____   **e** $\frac{1}{5}$ of 10 = _____   **f** $\frac{1}{4}$ of 4 = _____

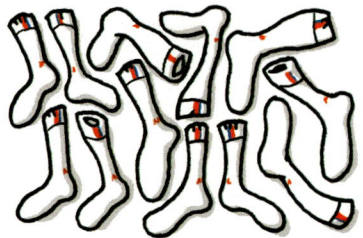 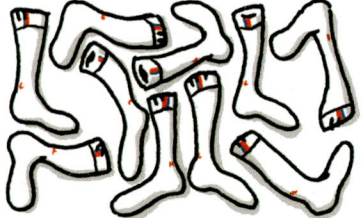 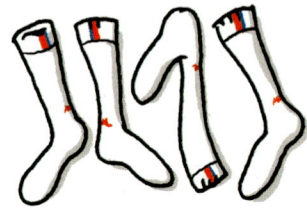

Some football strips are designed in halves or in quarters.

1 Colour these kits to show halves and quarters.

2 Colour the grids.

a Colour ¼ blue.

Colour ¼ red.

What fraction is coloured? _____

b Colour ½ red.

Colour ¼ blue.

What fraction is coloured? _____

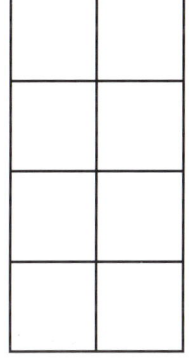

This is a strange strip. Do you think any Premier League team would like to try it?

5 Complete the strip.

- Colour half the spots blue.
- Colour a quarter of them green.
- Colour the rest yellow.
- What fraction of the spots are yellow? _____

Pre-match Multiplication Tables

training

Look at this multiplication table.

×	0	1	2	3	4	5	6	7	8	9	10
2	0	2	4	6	8	10	12	14	16	18	20
5	0	5	10	15	20	25	30	35	40	45	50
10	0	10	20	30	40	50	60	70	80	90	100

5 × 4 is the same as 4 × 5.
It does not matter which way you multiply them.

practice

A Write the numbers that leave each turnstile.

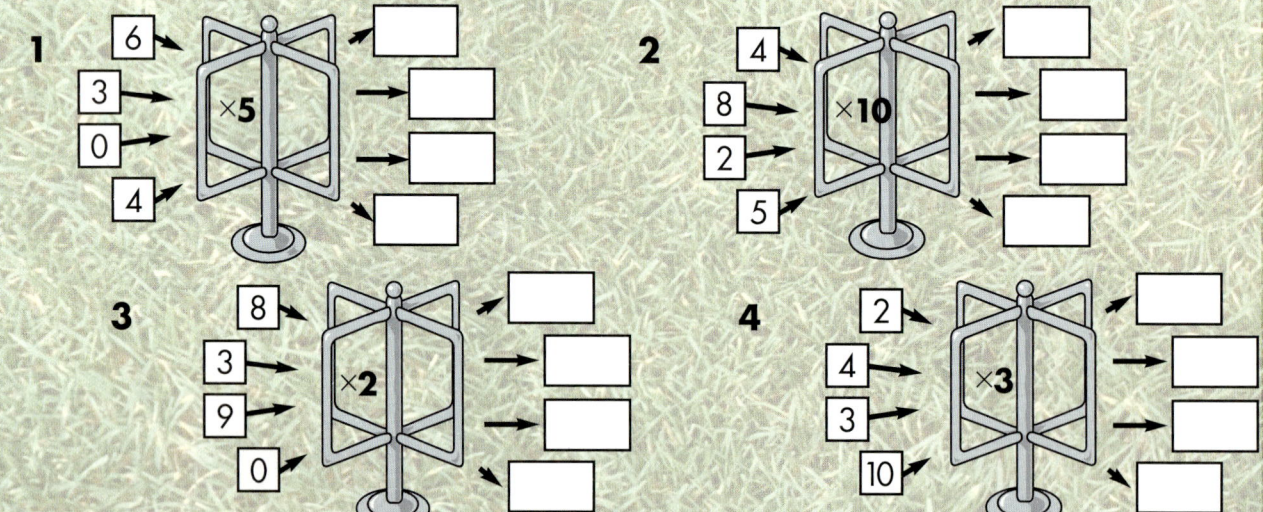

B Fill in the missing numbers.

1 ☐ × 3 = 15   2 8 × ☐ = 16   3 5 × 4 = ☐

4 7 × ☐ = 14   5 ☐ × 3 = 12   6 7 × 10 = ☐

Arsenal FC v Valencia

Match 3

Write the answers.

1. 7 × 2 = 14
2. 4 × 3 = 12
3. 5 × 10 = 50
4. 6 × 5 = 30
5. 3 × 6 = 18
6. 10 × 7 = 70

HALF-TIME

Write the missing numbers.

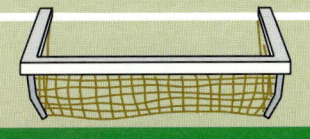

7. 8 × 2 = 16
8. 4 × 5 = 20
9. 9 × 16 = 90
10. 3 × 2 = 6
11. 7 × ☐ = 14
12. ☐ × 3 = 21

Total: ☐ out of 12

Colour the bar on the right to find out how many goals you've scored for Arsenal.

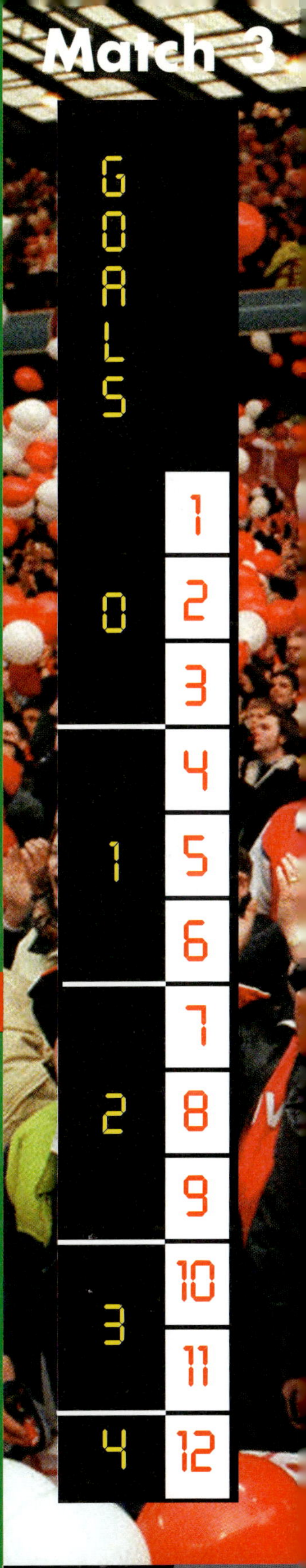

ARSENAL FC ☐

VALENCIA 1

Now turn to page 28 and fill in the score on the Super-League Results Table.

Odds and Evens

You need:

2 dice

2 counters

How to play

- Put a counter on the centre circle.
- Roll the dice and multiply the numbers together.
- Follow the directions for an even or an odd answer.
- How many moves does it take you to score a goal?

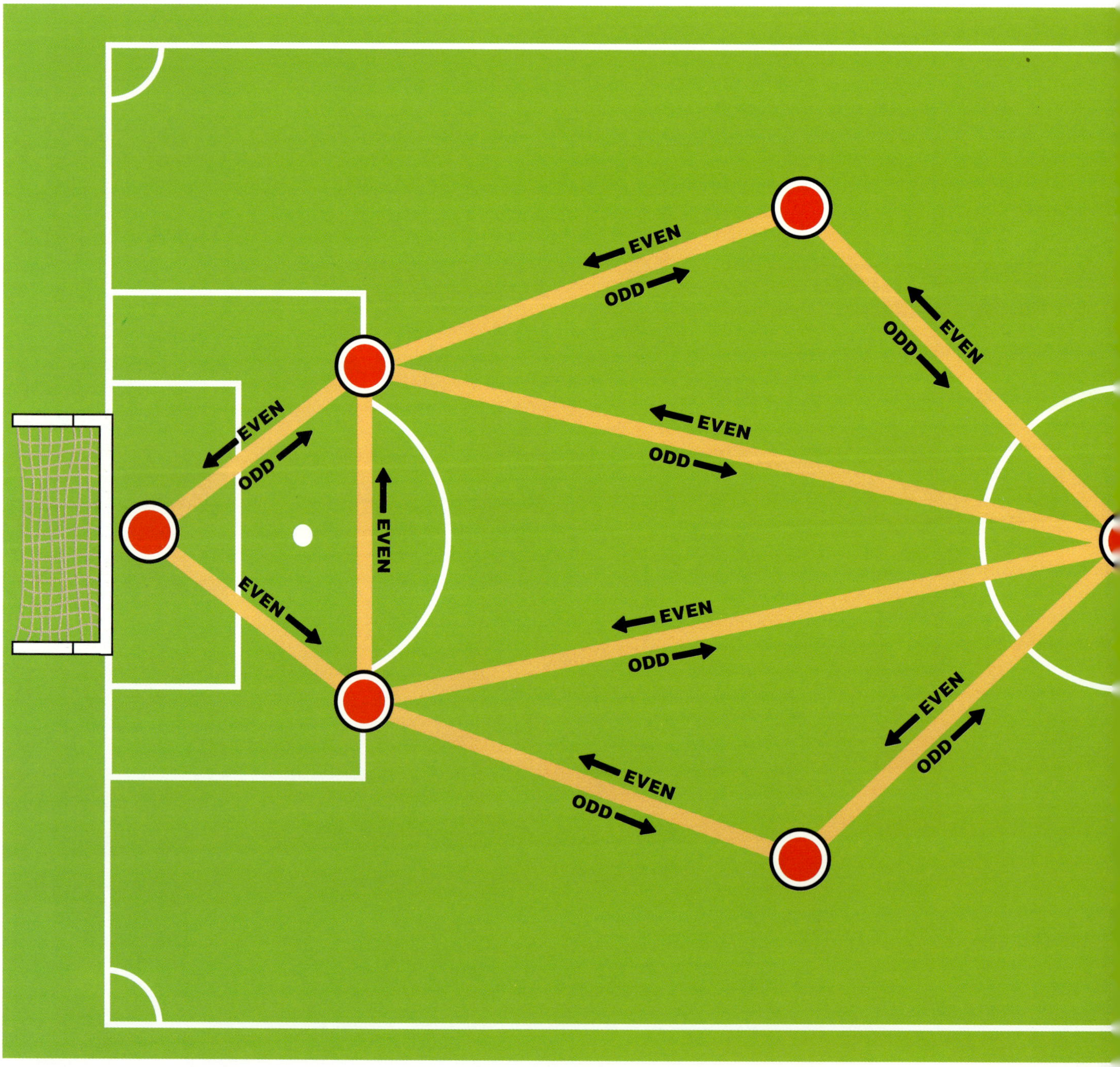

16

Aim: The winner is the first player to score 3 goals.

- Play a match against another player. Place both counters on the centre circle and take turns to move. Both players score at the same end. The first player to score three goals is the winner.

- Once you have kicked off, both counters cannot be in the same space. If you cannot go, you miss a turn.

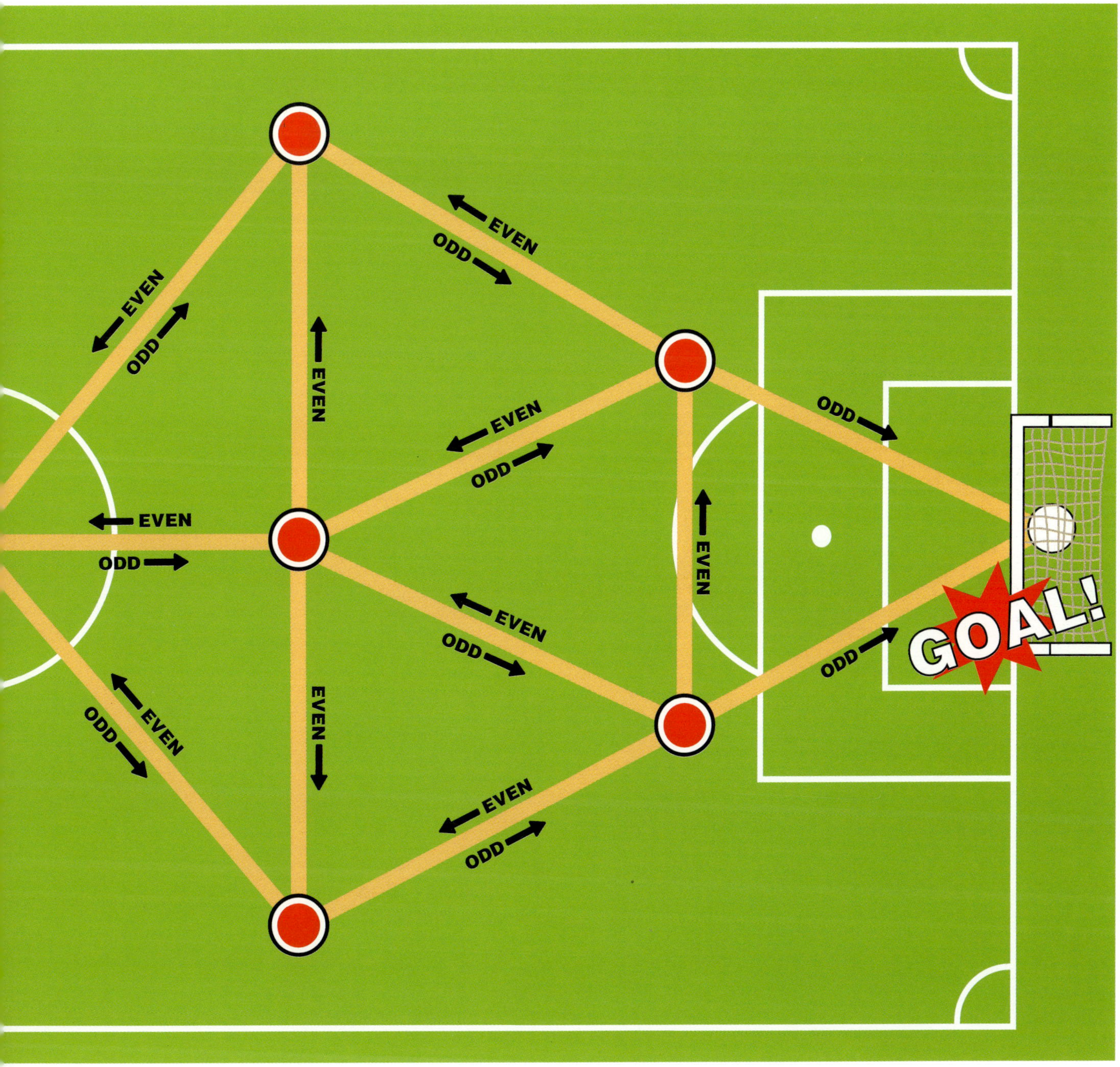

Pre-match Money

training

Working out **change** can be easy.
You must be able to make amounts up to £1.00.

A sticker costs 35p. This is how you can work out the change from £1.

35p → Make up to next 10p → + 5p → 40p → Make up to £1.00 → + 60p → change 65p

practice

A Write the totals.

1) 5p + £10 + 20p = _____

2) 5p + £10 + £20 + 20p = _____

3) 10p + £10 + £10 + 20p = _____

4) 5p + 20p + 50p + £10 = _____

Write the change.

5) £10, price £7.50 = _____

6) £5, price £3.75 = _____

7) £2, price 90p = _____

8) £1, price 85p = _____

B 1 Which three coins total 26p?

_____

2 Which three coins total 62p?

_____

18

Arsenal FC v Bayern Munich

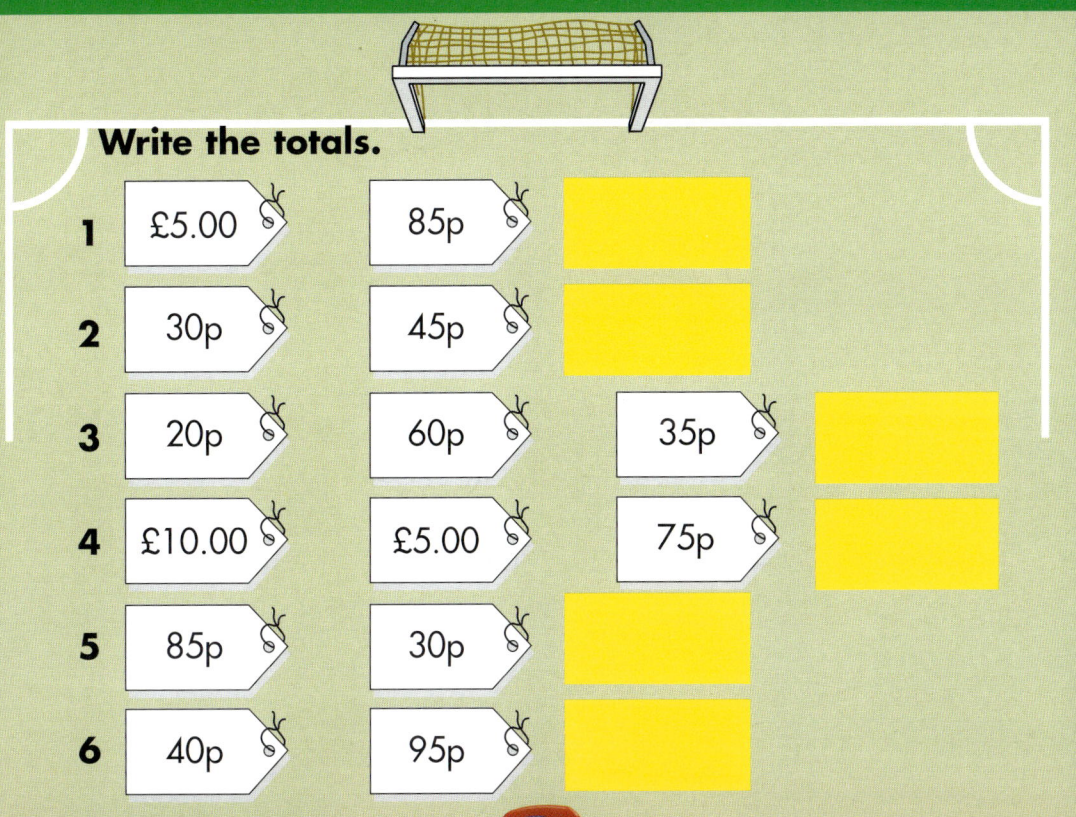

Match 4

Write the totals.

1. £5.00   85p   _____
2. 30p   45p   _____
3. 20p   60p   35p   _____
4. £10.00 £5.00 75p   _____
5. 85p   30p   _____
6. 40p   95p   _____

HALF-TIME

Write the change from £1.00 for each of these prices.

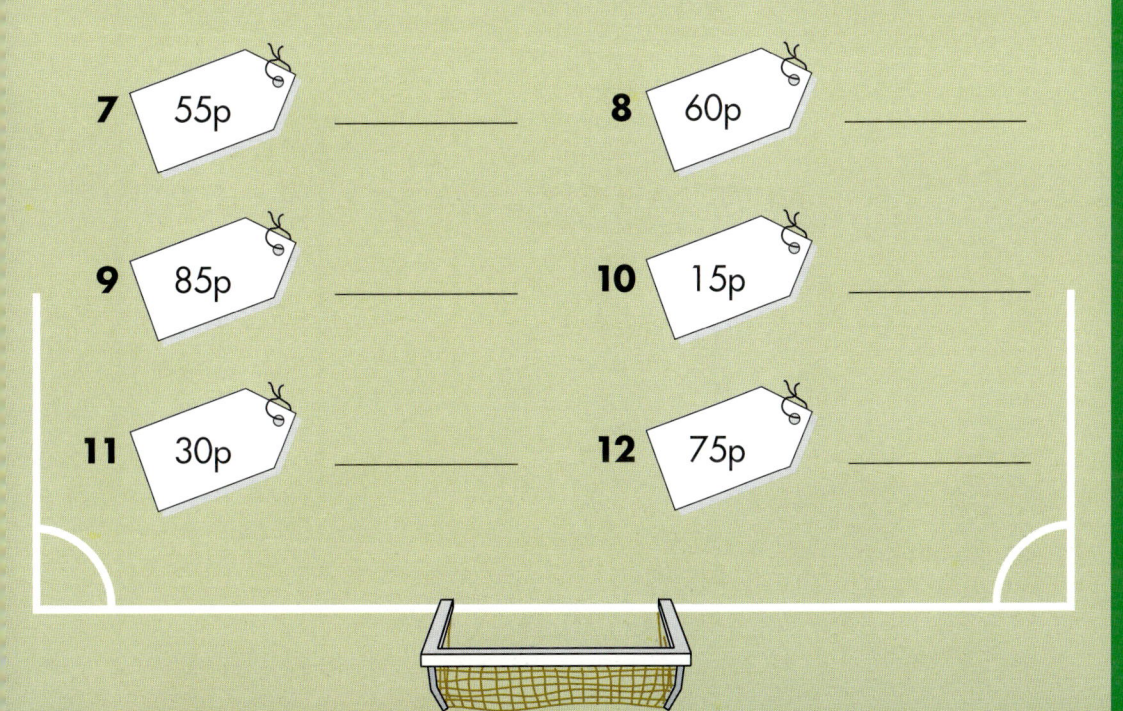

7. 55p   _____   8. 60p   _____
9. 85p   _____   10. 15p   _____
11. 30p   _____   12. 75p   _____

GOALS

Arsenal FC	
Bayern Munich	2

Total: _____ out of 12

Colour the bar on the right to find out how many goals you've scored for Arsenal.

Now turn to page 28 and fill in the score on the Super-League Results Table.

Highbury

Arsenal play at Highbury in north London. The stadium holds about 38,500 supporters. They plan to move to a new larger stadium, to cater for more fans, within the next five years. Shapes can be spotted everywhere at Highbury.

rectangle
circle
rhombus
parallelogram
triangle
hexagon
square
semicircle

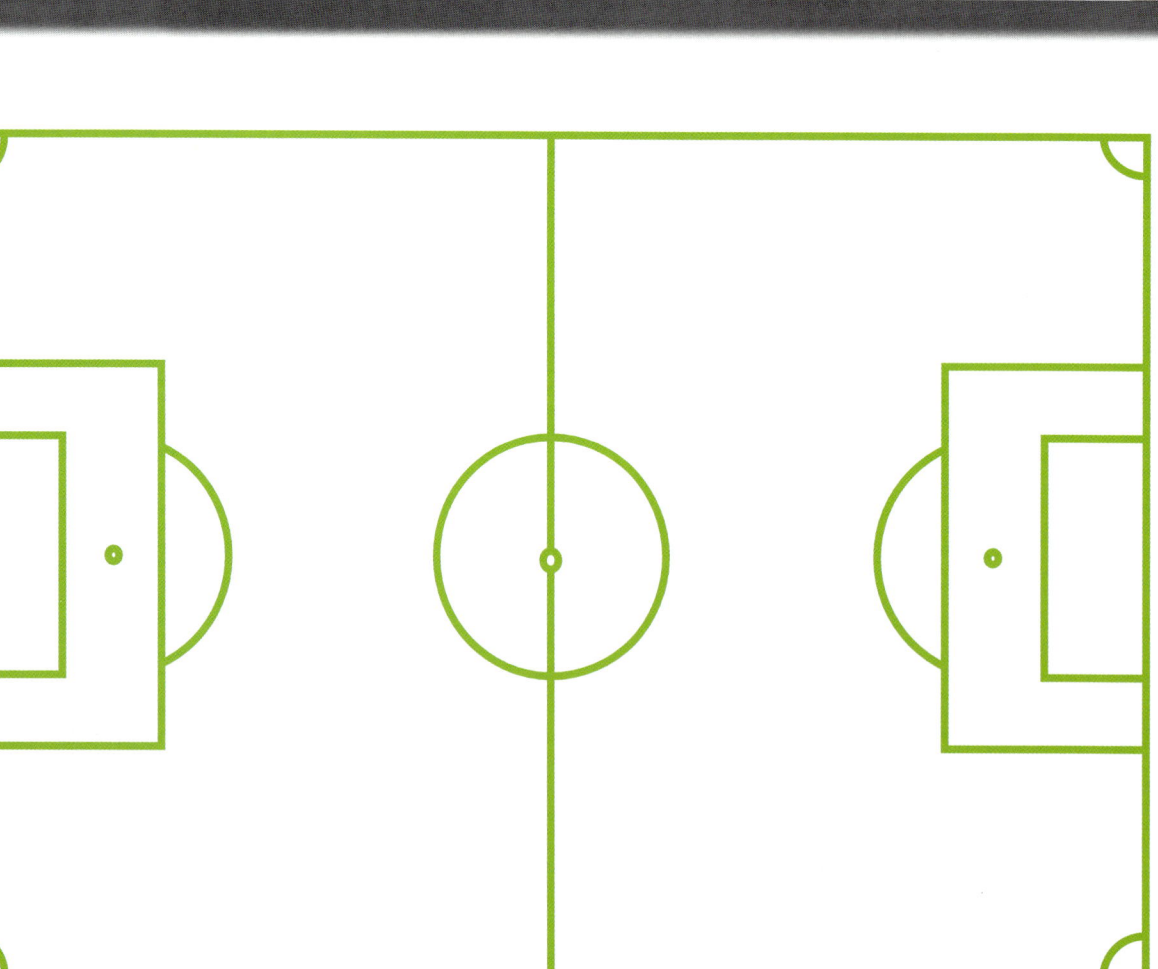

1 Name these shapes.

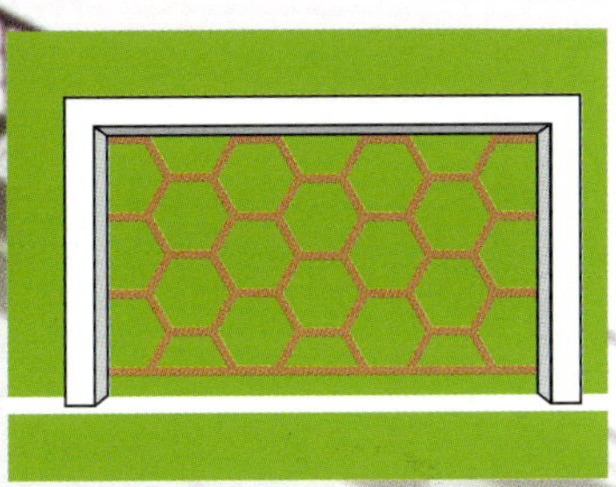

a  _____   b _____

c  _____   d _____

Look at the pitch on the left.

2 a Colour all the right angles on the pitch.

  b How many right angles did you find? _____

3 Colour the right angles on these shapes.

Did you know ... ?
In 1932, Arsenal tube station was named after the club. It was previously known as Gillespie Road.

 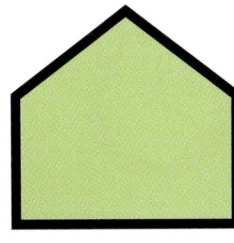  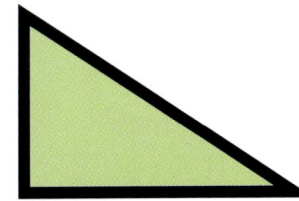

EXTRA TIME

4 Divide the grid into four parts. Each part must have one of each shape.

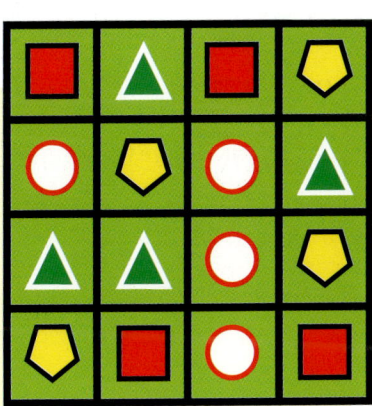

21

Pre-match Time

training

The **minute hand** tells you how many **minutes past the hour**.

```
                    o'clock
   55 minutes past          5 minutes past
   50 minutes past          10 minutes past
   45 minutes past          15 minutes past
   40 minutes past          20 minutes past
   35 minutes past          25 minutes past
              30 minutes past
```

practice

A Write the times shown on these clocks.

1.   2.   3.   4.

___   ___   ___   ___

5.   6.   7.   8.

___   ___   ___   ___

B Do you know these time facts?

1. How many minutes are in 1 hour? _____

2. How many days are there in April? _____

3. What time is half an hour before 4.15? _____

4. Which month follows October? _____

Arsenal FC v Ajax

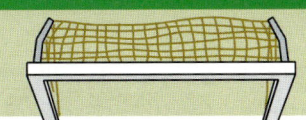

Write the times.

1 _____ minutes past _____

2 _____ minutes past _____

3 _____ minutes past _____

4 _____ minutes past _____

5 _____ minutes past _____

6 _____ minutes past _____

HALF-TIME

Draw the hands on the clocks for these times.

7 4.05

8 9.35

9 2.45

10 11.20

11 6.55

12 8.15

Total: ☐ out of 12

Colour the bar on the right to find out how many goals you've scored for Arsenal.

Match 5

GOALS

0 — 1 — 2 — 3 — 4

1 — 2 — 3 — 4 — 5 — 6 — 7 — 8 — 9 — 10 — 11 — 12

ARSENAL FC ☐

AJAX 1

Now turn to page 28 and fill in the score on the Super-League Results Table.

The Team

Arsenal were runners-up in the 1999–2000 season. The table on the right gives some information about 16 players from last season's team and how well they did.

A winning team.

1 Use the table to answer these.

   a Who was top scorer for the season? _____

   b Which two players played the least Premiership matches? _____
   _____

   c Who made six times the appearances of Stefan Malz? _____

   d What was the total number of goals scored by the two highest goal scorers?
   _____

   e Who made three fewer appearances than Patrick Vieira?
   _____

   f What was the total number of appearances made by Kanu and Dennis Bergkamp?
   _____

24

Player	Premiership Appearances	Premiership Goals
Tony Adams	21	0
Dennis Bergkamp	28	6
Lee Dixon	28	4
Gilles Grimandi	28	2
Thierry Henry	31	17
Kanu	31	12
Martin Keown	27	1
Fredrik Ljungberg	26	6
Oleg Luzhny	21	0
Stefan Malz	5	1
Ray Parlour	30	1
David Seaman	24	0
Silvinho	32	1
Matthew Upson	8	0
Patrick Vieira	30	2
Nelson Vivas	5	0

Score!

Lee Dixon scored 4 goals in 28 appearances.

This can be written as $\frac{4}{28}$ or simplified: $\frac{2}{14} \rightarrow \div 2 \rightarrow \frac{1}{7}$

So, on average, Lee Dixon scored 1 goal in every 7 games.

2 Work these out in the same way:

  a Gilles Grimandi

  b Fredrick Ljungberg

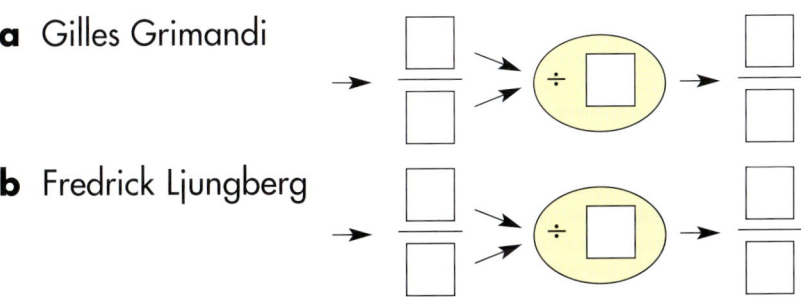

Pre-match Rounding and Reading Scales

training

Rounding to the nearest 10
When you are rounding to the **nearest 10**, look at the **last digit**. If it is 5 or more, round up. If not, round down.

37 ⟶ Round up to 40
144 ⟶ Round down to 140
365 ⟶ Round up to 370

Rounding to the nearest 100
When you are rounding to the **nearest 100**, look at the **last 2 digits**. If they make 50 or more, round up. If not, round down.

572 ⟶ Round up to 600
839 ⟶ Round down to 800
650 ⟶ Round up to 700

practice

A Round each number to the nearest 10.

1 74 ⟶ ______ **2** 96 ⟶ ______ **3** 145 ⟶ ______

4 307 ⟶ ______ **5** 294 ⟶ ______

Round each number to the nearest 100.

6 460 ⟶ ______ **7** 348 ⟶ ______ **8** 709 ⟶ ______

9 850 ⟶ ______ **10** 134 ⟶ ______

B Read these scales. Round each one to the nearest 100 g.

[ ] rounded to ⟶ [ ]

[ ] rounded to ⟶ [ ]

[ ] rounded to ⟶ [ ]

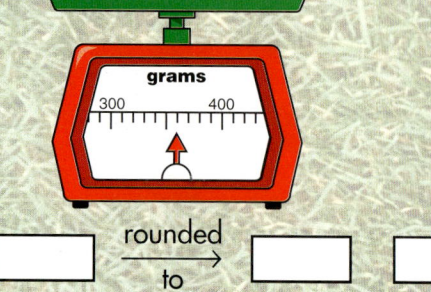

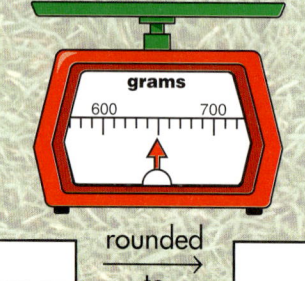

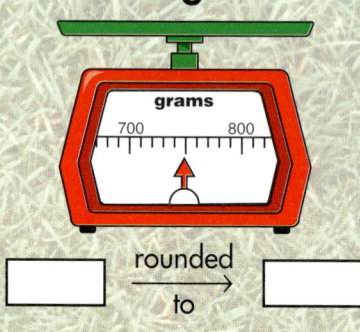

Arsenal FC v Malmo

Match 6

Round these to the nearest 10.

1 86 → _____   2 107 → _____

3 245 → _____   4 614 → _____

5 956 → _____   6 203 → _____

HALF-TIME

Round each scale to the nearest 100 g.

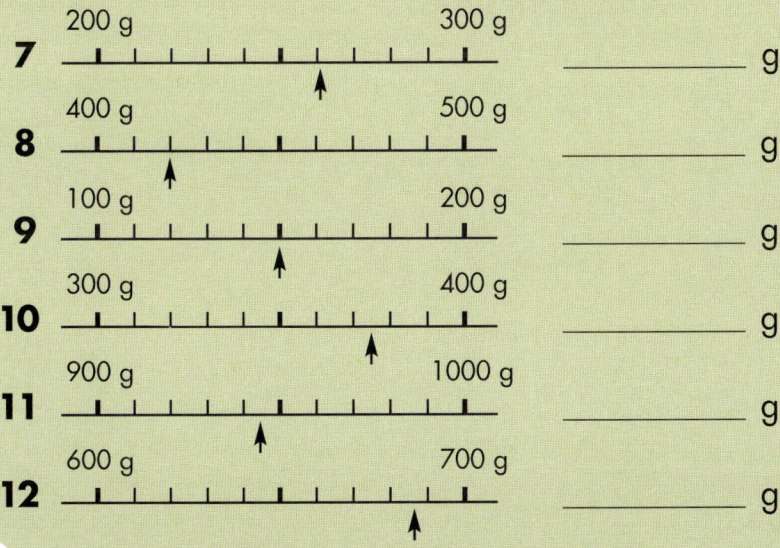

7 _____ g

8 _____ g

9 _____ g

10 _____ g

11 _____ g

12 _____ g

Total: [   ] out of 12

Colour the bar on the right to find out how many goals you've scored for Arsenal.

Arsenal FC [   ]

Malmo 0

Now turn to page 28 and fill in the score on the Super-League Results Table.

Super-League Results

MATCH 1

Arsenal FC	3	Monaco	2
Malmo	3	Valencia	2
Lazio	0	Ajax	2

MATCH 2

Arsenal FC	6	Lazio	3
Valencia	2	Monaco	2
Malmo	2	B Munich	2

MATCH 3

Valencia	1	Arsenal FC	2
Lazio	1	Monaco	0
Ajax	4	B Munich	3

MATCH 4

B Munich	2	Arsenal FC	4
Valencia	1	Lazio	3
Malmo	0	Ajax	2

MATCH 5

Ajax	1	Arsenal FC	5
B Munich	1	Lazio	1
Malmo	4	Monaco	0

MATCH 6

Arsenal FC	1	Malmo	0
Monaco	0	Ajax	0
Valencia	0	B Munich	2

MATCH 7

B Munich	1	Monaco	3
Valencia	1	Ajax	1
Malmo	0	Lazio	1

Super-League Tables

Enter the score for each match.

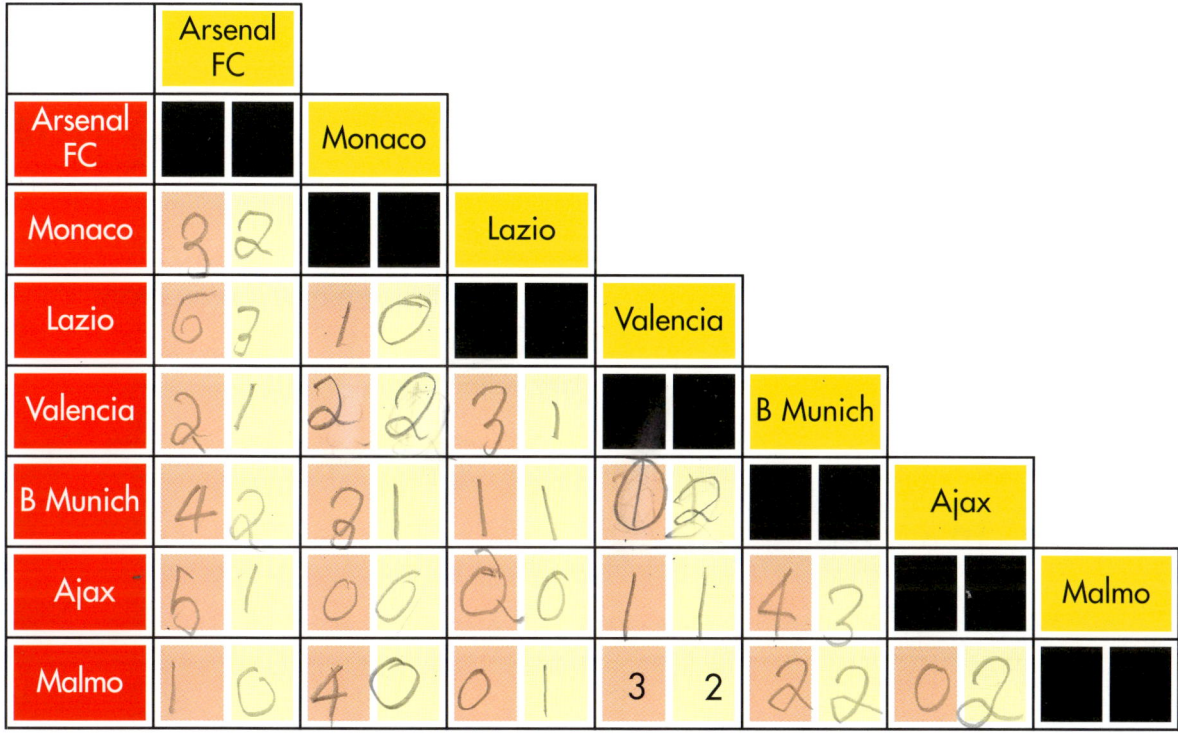

Complete the league table when all the matches are finished.

| Win | 3 pts | Draw | 1 pt | Lose | 0 pts |

Team	Played	Won	Drew	Lost	For	Against	Goal diff	Points
Arsenal FC	6	6	0	0			21	18
Monaco	6	1	1	4			7	4
Lazio	6	3	1	2			9	10
Valencia	6	0	1	5			7	1
B Munich	6	1	2	3			4	5
Ajax	6	3	2	1			10	11
Malmo	6	2	3	1			9	9

Champions  Runners-up ajax

ANSWERS

The Club 4–5
1 38 **2** 7 **3** 4 **4** 1996 **5** 27 **6** 70
7 Manchester United – 179; Chelsea – 53; Newcastle United – 175; Liverpool – 124;
8 Bergkamp – 138; Henry – 173. Henry's total is greater.

Match 1 Place Value 6–7
Pre-match
A 7000 seven thousand
  17   seventeen
  71   seventy-one
  701   seven hundred and one
  77   seventy-seven
  7010 seven thousand and ten
  170   one hundred and seventy
  70   seventy
B **1** 80 **2** 200, 60 **3** 2000, 40 **4** 700, 9

The Match
1 80 **2** 410 **3** 1045 **4** 63 **5** 891 **6** 742
7 60 **8** 400 **9** 200 **10** 8 **11** 600
12 8000

The Players 8–9
1 February
2 8, 4
3 Ljungberg: (1,4) (6,1); Bergkamp: (1,3) (9,3); Upson: (2,3) (10,4); Cole: (2,2) (9,1); Vivas: (2,1) (8,3); Dixon: (4,4) (7,4); Barrett: (4,1) (8,2); Grimandi: (5,4) (9,2); Keown: (5,2) (7,3); Lukic: (6,4) (8,1); Seaman: (6,3) (10,1); Adams (7,1) (9,4); Wiltord (1,2) (3,2); Malz (4,3) (7,2)

4 Crossword with answers: SEAMAN, STEVENAGE, BCO, COKA, LUKIC, ADAMS, PARLOUR, GER, RULL, HENRY, VIEIRA, MALZ

5 O'Leary (find out more about David O'Leary).

Match 2 Addition and Subtraction ...10–11
Pre-match
A **1** 19 **2** 13 **3** 23 **4** 27 **5** 28 **6** 6 **7** 5
  8 3 **9** 13 **10** 8
B **1** 18 **2** 20 **3** 11 **4** 14

The Match
1 23 **2** 8 **3** 22 **4** 9 **5** 33 **6** 24 **7** 21
8 8 **9** 27 **10** 32p **11** 21 **12** 4

The Strip 12–13
1 Check the colouring shows halves and quarters.
2 a $\frac{1}{2}$ **b** $\frac{3}{4}$
3 Check the socks are matched correctly.
4 a 4 **b** 3 **c** 5 **d** 4 **e** 2 **f** 1
5 $\frac{1}{4}$ are yellow

Match 3 Multiplication Tables 14–15
Pre-match
A **1** 30 15 0   20
  2 40 80 20 50
  3 16 6   18 0
  4 6   12 9   30
B **1** 5 **2** 2 **3** 20 **4** 2 **5** 4 **6** 70

The Match
1 14 **2** 12 **3** 50 **4** 30 **5** 18 **6** 70
7 2 **8** 4 **9** 10 **10** 3 **11** 2 **12** 7

Match 4 Money 18–19
Pre-match
A **1** £10.25 **2** £30.25 **3** £20.30 **4** £10.75
  5 £2.50 **6** £1.25 **7** £1.10 **8** 15p
B **1** 20p coin, 5p coin and 1p coin
  2 50p coin, 10p coin and 2p coin

The Match
1 £5.85 **2** 75p **3** £1.15 **4** £15.75
5 £1.15 **6** £1.35 **7** 45p **8** 40p **9** 15p
10 85p **11** 70p **12** 25p

Highbury 20–21
1 a Hexagons **b** Semicircle **c** Rectangles
  d Circle
2 a Check the right angles. **b** 32
3

4

Match 5 Time 22–23

Pre-match
A 1 5 minutes past 5   2 55 minutes past 9
   3 30 minutes past 8   4 40 minutes past 2
   5 5 minutes past 3   6 35 minutes past 3
   7 8 o'clock   8 45 minutes past 5
B 1 60 minutes   2 30 days   3 3.45
   4 November

The Match
1 15 minutes past 4
2 35 minutes past 8
3 45 minutes past 6
4 10 minutes past 11
5 55 minutes past 1
6 40 minutes past 2

7  8  9

10  11  12

The Team 24–25
1 a Henry   b Malz and Vivas
  c Parlour   d 29   e Keown   f 59
2 a $\frac{2}{28}$, 2, $\frac{1}{14}$,   Gilles Grimandi scored 1 goal in every 14 games.

  b $\frac{6}{26}$, 2, $\frac{3}{13}$,   Fredrick Ljungberg scored 3 goals in every 13 games

Match 6
Rounding and Reading Scales 26–27

Pre-match
A 1 70   2 100   3 150   4 310   5 290
  6 500   7 300   8 700   9 900   10 100
B 360 g   300 g;   650 g   700 g;
   750 g   800 g

The Match
1 90   2 110   3 250   4 610   5 960
6 200   7 300 g   8 400 g   9 200 g
10 400 g   11 900 g   12 700 g

Arsenal FC Double Club

The Double Club is an exciting new football and education venture developed by 'Arsenal in the Community'. Inspired by Arsenal's Double 1998 League and Cup triumph, the Club involves 45 minutes of after school fun with literacy and numeracy study support and 45 minutes of football coaching. Volunteers from local secondary schools help out with the Clubs. Pupils complete a 24-week course to ensure that they receive the best tuition on and off the field.

If your primary, middle or secondary school is interested in receiving further information about the Double Club please contact Alan Sefton at: Arsenal Football Club
e-mail: bnicholas@arsenal.co.uk   Tel: 020 7704 4140   Fax: 020 7704 4001

Collect the set

Each book introduces new skills and harder challenges. Collect all 8 and be an English and Maths champion.

Arsenal FC English Books 1–4

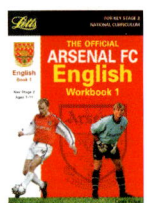 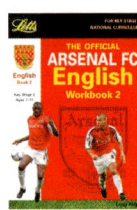 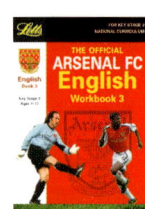 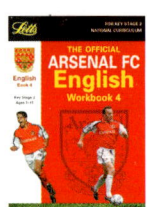

Arsenal FC Maths Books 1–4

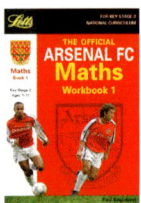 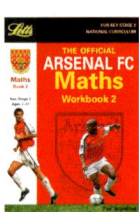 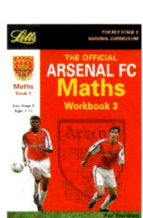 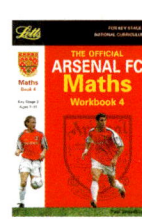

For all the latest news, views and information on

Arsenal FC

visit the official Arsenal website:

www.arsenal.com

Arsenal Football Club PLC
Arsenal Stadium, Highbury, London N5 1BU

Letts Educational, Aldine House, Aldine Place, London W12 8AW
Tel: 020 8740 2266 Fax: 020 8743 8451 E-mail: mail@lettsed.co.uk
Website: www.letts-education.com

Every effort has been made to trace copyright holders and obtain their permission for the use of copyright material. The authors and publishers will gladly receive information enabling them to rectify any error or omission in subsequent editions.

All facts are correct at time of going to press.

Published 2001
© Letts Educational Ltd
Author: Paul Broadbent
Editorial and Design: Moondisks Ltd, Cambridge
Illustrations: Joel Morris
Colour Reprographics: PDQ Digital Media Solutions Ltd, Bungay

Our thanks to the players and staff at Arsenal Football Club.
Photographs copyright Arsenal Football Club and Colorsport.

All rights reserved. No part of this publication may be reproduced, stored in a retrieval system, or transmitted, in any form or by any means, electronic, mechanical, photocopying, recording or otherwise, without the prior permission of Letts Educational.

British Library Cataloguing in Publication Data
A CIP record for this book is available from the British Library.
ISBN 1-85805-887-2

Printed in the UK.

Letts Educational Limited is a member of Granada Learning Limited, part of the Granada Media Group.